AHLUMBA HARRIS

Release & Unleash

AHLUMBA HARRIS

Release & Unleash
The Path to Greatness

AHLUMBA HARRIS

Copyright © 2015 Ahlumba Harris

Edited by: Chrissy Cutting

Cover Art by: Andy Monk

All rights reserved. No part of this book may be reproduced or transmitted for commercial or non commercial use in any form by any means, electronic or mechanical, including photocopying, recording, or by any information storage and retrieval system without written approval from the Author.

Unless otherwise listed All Scripture references comes from The King James Version Bible

Library of Congress Control Number: 2015903135

ISBN: 099158791X
ISBN-13: 978-0991587919

To order additional copies of this book, contact:

Inspired2Prosper International LLC
contactus@inspired2prosper.com
www.ahlumba.com

DEDICATION

To every individual who has touched and blessed my life
knowingly and unknowingly, I thank you.

CONTENTS

Acknowledgments	i
Prelude Release	1
The Journey	5
Not As Planned	7
Do You	9
Paved	11
Will I Ever	13
Excuses Yield Nothing	15
Unto You I Will Not Do	16
Selfish Boy & Girl	18
Unworthy	20
Dream Killer	22
You Have No Idea	23
Strength In The Midst	25
How Much Longer	27
Remain The Course	29
I Wondered Why	31

Press On	33		
You Need Me Not I You	34	I Looked And Saw Me	54
Trust & Believe	35	Once There Was None	56
Shamed By Need	37	The Dawn Is What I See	57
Will It Ever Be	39	No One But Me	58
Could Not	40	Thanksgiving	59
Keep The Faith	43	Idle Heart	60
Fresh Start	45	Sleeping Giant	61
Colleagues We Will Be	46	Change What You See	62
Think No Less Of Me	48	Never Give Up	63
Never Again	50	Everything Has A Beginning	65
It's Turning Around	51	Can't Get Enough	73
Unable	53	About Ahlumba	75

ACKNOWLEDGMENTS

I thank The Father, The Son, and the Holy Spirit who are three yet one…whom without none of this would be possible.

Dana Williams thank you for being a blessing in my life.

My accountability coach Malika Humphries; thank you for believing in me enough to freely invest your gifts and talent into the success of my own.

Bahia Carson if it was not for you blessing me with the use of your laptop (after my own crashed) I would not have completed this book.

My family and every individual who has touched and blessed my life knowingly and unknowingly, I thank you.

AHLUMBA HARRIS

THE BEGINNING

There is no brokenness that you can experience that God cannot mend, hurt He cannot heal, lack He cannot prosper, sorrow He cannot turn to joy, or problem that He cannot turn around to your good!
~Ahlumba

RELEASED INTO THE UNEXPECTED

The day that I sat and poured out my heart never did I realize that in this way I would eventually impart. During what I believe to be some of my most difficult times, I would sit in my room and cry while wondering how much longer would this struggle endure? The anguish of having to depend on others due to my financial instability, the lack of ability to maintain my home, the constant fear of losing everything I worked so hard to gain, and the pressure to succeed weighed heavily on me.

Although the dream of greater purpose and a desire for a life of more abundance burned inside of me, I still wondered "Was pursuing this dream the right decision?" and "Is all this difficulty and struggle worth it?" Ever unknowing of how I would make it from one day to the next, my days became desolate.

Cast down and on the verge of defeat, I began to change the way I started my mornings with the hope that surely, this would be the day that all the years of labor, hard work, seeds planted, and consistency would finally pay off. Yet nothing seemed to ever yield in my favor.

In my greatest of efforts, it was as if nothing I did was ever good enough. No matter how hard I worked or tried, consistent continual success remained elusive. As a result of what seemed to be my constant failure, self-sabotaging thoughts seemed to overtake my defeatist spirit. However, deep down I knew the negative could not remain, for my dreams were as a bubbling brook that refused to be contained. Successful is what I wanted to be, but that success was so much harder to obtain than I ever thought it would be.

I yearned to unleash all the greatness that I had no doubt to be inside of me. To release the pain of all the sorrow I could not help but feel, relinquish the fear of the constant "what if's" that whispered in my ear, to let go of the anger I felt due to everything always being so hard won, and most importantly of all free my at times mustard seed hope by not only trusting but also believing that my situation would indeed turn around.

"Due to the negative evidence of my current situation, it was increasingly difficult to believe that the dream that I hoped to achieve would actually one day manifest."

With no one around to truly express the rapidly depleting faith and belief I was experiencing, I made the decision to believe in the very God I had begun to doubt. Many mornings, evenings, and nights I poured out to Him all the pain, fear, disbelief, and anxiety that held me bound. I was angry. Nevertheless, he had mercy and gifted me with peace. I was confused with an inability to express myself properly yet He gave me words of expression. Through God, I was able to let go. He allowed me the grace to use the pain of my past to help create the steps to my future.

Despite the doubt, struggle, and the virtual absence of evidence to support that I would ever succeed, I made the choice to continue moving forward by refusing to give up. Not due to any greatness or understanding of my own but due solely to the grace, compassion, understanding, constant forgiveness, love, and newness of mind that God saw fit to bestow daily upon me.

I who had nothing was able to do something. I who wavered and faltered was not given up on. I who at times sat in the dark and cried was uplifted. And I who thought what I had to offer was not enough was shown that no matter what, God will not allow the appropriate connection earlier than it is intended nor will He allow it to be birth before its time.

"No matter how badly we want it to be, we cannot force wrong timing to be correct."

On my path to greater victory, financial freedom, spiritual wholeness and purpose, I have learned that God is able to turn around **ANY** situation. No matter how impossible it may seem, if you will have the faith and trust to believe even when faced with evidence of a life of demise, defeat, lack, and or loneliness I implore you to trust that God can and will complete the good work He has begun in your life… for troubles do not, will not, and cannot always last!

I literally stepped out on sheer faith by choosing to pursue what I believed in – and I was rewarded with purpose. It was not always easy. In fact, it has been downright troublesome and difficult. However it is due to the adversity that I have faced that I have been given a platform for without it there would be no success. I have learned that trouble and struggle will not and cannot last forever!

"Release and Unleash" is my way of sharing what happens following the decision to accept what one believes to be their purpose when all the hype of "Dare to dream, Live your best life now, and You can do it" has flickered and died.

Despite the struggles, doubts, and fears that I faced the Lord saw fit to allow me the strength and faith to overcome it all. It is for that reason that I strive in everything that I do and with every fiber of my being to encourage, uplift, and empower those who are faced with nothingness and no hope but still have a willingness to achieve with the tools that the Lord has given me.

If you refuse to lose how then can you ever fail? You will win!

THE JOURNEY

It's not easy stepping out the box of what is considered the acceptable norm. However, if we refuse to give our fear room to bind us, we will then be free to do what we once thought to be impossible.

AHLUMBA HARRIS

NOT AS PLANNED

The Lord moved me to write in another direction,
One I did not foresee nor one that I expected.
He has filled me up, now I must release
All the words he has put inside of me.
Following his lead has become a must,
For where would I be without his trust?
Probably broken stuck or lost
Would have been my trough.
So when he calls to you as he did unto me,
It is a must that you be
A willing vessel, ready to receive.
And you will constantly gain
Due to your willingness to receive.

I had just completed "Fat Girl Pick Your Head Up" and was on the verge of completing another book that I previously began "Letters From A Desperate Heart" when I began to hear in my spirit several rhyming combinations that seemed to express the current emotions, thoughts, and feelings that I was experiencing.

The words filled me up to capacity and danced in my

mind until I had to open up a new page by which I allowed myself the freedom to release everything. I was taken by word combinations that refused to cease. It did not take much longer before I realized that God was positioning me to go down a path I never expected.
I was creating a story through poetry.

Though I dabbled in it on occasion, it never occurred to me that I would ever be able to express myself entirely through rhythmic form. I was in total amazement that this came from me.

Don't ever put too much stock into your own preparation for when you think you have a plan, God comes along with a greater one.

DO YOU?

Do you really want to succeed,
Was the question asked of me.
Are you beyond the point of caring
About what others will say or think?
For you better believe
Laughter, pointing, and mockery
Will certainly ensue
Because they have no vision.
So why should you?
Are you willing to succeed despite the cost?
Burning the night oil while they plan their days off?
Are you willing to pay the price that success
requires?
If it demanded you take a beating,
Would you still get up swinging?
I don't know about him or her,
But my night without lights let me know
That I don't have the luxury to continue to start
And then let go.
This journey will be completed until the end
Then you will be wondering
What was my question again?

How badly did I really want to succeed? Was I willing to go the distance at the expense of my pride? Was I willing to sacrifice and do without due to this dream that I so badly wanted to achieve? Would I keep going when all I wanted was relief from the habitual lack, chastisement, and disbelieve?

Faced with the possibility of never receiving what I worked so long and hard to achieve, I knew that in no way could I allow any circumstance of my life to negatively deter me from continuing this journey I set out upon. I would succeed!

PAVED BECAUSE OF PERSISTENCE

I stepped out with no one to show me.
Not knowing where to turn,
no one willing to mold me.
Mistakes I made. Yes, quite a few.
But in-spite of them, I continued to press through.
The trail I walked was non-existent
Until I decided to make the brick
That created the path of my current existence.
Dug by faith, tempered with tears,
And molded by every dream that I hoped to fulfill.
My building blocks have not always been easy,
But sometimes the valley of death is required
Before you can reach the beauty of life
That is considered to be your Eden.

When I made the choice to pursue my dream, I reached out to several individuals but none of them were willing to guide or direct me. I was not shown the proper way or format to write, publish, market, promote, or build a business. Nonetheless, I refused to allow that to stop me.

I was determined. I did what was in my heart and tried to imitate those that inspired me. Constantly the Lord gave me the strength to create my own path to success. So yes, mistakes, mishaps, and a lot of "that's not how it's done" were what I encountered, but I have learned to enjoy coloring outside the occasional line.

WILL I EVER

I am overwhelmed with thoughts of will I ever
While the walls that is my life,
Continue to shackle me.
Feeling incapable, still I try to break free.
Accosted I am from every direction,
With voices of doubt
And meaningful reflection.
To do this would take a great amount.
So how do you propose to bring it about?
With no clear direction
Not even a route.
I succumb to the pressure of my suffocating thoughts
by embracing the walls that have created my drought.
Now left in a rut,
I begin to wonder anew.
Always pondering what is the right thing to do,
My heart tells me one thing
But my circumstance reveals another.
So I decide to be logical,
Because that is what's expected of you.

Dreams are beautiful, and they are free but daily they appeared to punish me. I would go into work daily feeling like there was so much more than the current existence I was living. However, the only evidence I had was the dream and hope that resided in me.

Every time I encountered someone prospering in his or her gift, I would get excited then sad because I felt that time was only counting against me. I wanted to leave my job, I wanted to operate my business full-time, but the pressure to remain my current course got to me, so I made the decision to squash the voice that demanded that I risk it all.

EXCUSES YIELD NOTHING

I don't mean to be ugly.
I certainly don't mean to be unkind.
But frankly, I'm sick and tired
Of hearing you whine.
You say you have faith.
You say you believe.
Yet the words out your mouth
tends to mislead.
Either you go for it or you don't,
For at this point,
you are no more than a joke.

After being around one too many individuals who talked all the time but never did anything, I was tired of hearing the advice they gave to me when I saw how they declined to use it themselves. I refused to allow the reflection of their unfulfilled dreams to ripple across my own.

It is always easy to give advice when you are on the outside looking in. However, I was to the point of belief that if you were not being about it then please keep all of your wonderful advice to yourself.

UNTO YOU I WILL NOT DO

Support is fickle, I say this from the heart,
For where were you when I was falling apart?
Laughing, pointing, or maybe hoping I would fail.
Or better yet watching from afar...
Yes, way back behind that veil.
Silently you looked on or maybe you didn't care,
For you refused to offer any of your helping hands.
Yet you give your support with freedom and care
To people who don't even know you're there.
But let me make it then I'm sure you will appear
With your hands held out like you were always there.
Though I now know what you are all about.
Don't worry, I will not do the same to you.
But how can you change
If you have never been taught
That one day you will need help
And let's hope that you're not offered
A cold, selfish, dormant heart.

Lack of support from friends and family used to get under my skin. I mean, I was borderline bitter. It was hard to observe those you knew ignore and refuse to offer a helping hand, yet see them be a cheerleader for someone who did not know or care that they existed.

However, after bemoaning the lack of support for a couple of years, the Lord began to reveal and help me understand through the following scripture:

"Ye have heard that it hath been said, Thou shalt love thy neighbour, and hate thine enemy. 44 But I say unto you, Love your enemies, bless them that curse you, do good to them that hate you, and pray for them which despitefully use you, and persecute you; 45 That ye may be the children of your Father which is in heaven: for he maketh his sun to rise on the evil and on the good, and sendeth rain on the just and on the unjust. 46 For if ye love them which love you, what reward have ye? Do not even the publicans the same? 47 And if ye salute your brethren only, what do ye more than others? Do not even the publicans so?" Matthew 5:43-47

I learned that my anger towards those who offered me little to no support made me know better than them. For despite one's choices, whether they be favorable or not, the Christ in me requires that I demonstrate love by offering unto them what they refused me, doing in turn unto others as I would have them do unto me.

SELFISH BOY & GIRL

Snap I will not!
I must keep it all to myself.
As you flaunt your stuff
Without a care for the rest.
We can all tell when you are feeling yourself;
Fancy food, clothes, shopping
And all the rest.
But don't let you be down
Then you will appear
With needy hands and a listening heart.
Constantly you receive
Yes, you love to take
Yet there is no one that I know of
That you have ever helped to resuscitate.
Oh selfish girl and boy you are.
One day, I hope to see you give
As plenteously as you seem take.

This is one of the poems I wrote while in the midst of some extreme difficulty. I could barely pay my bills, had no money, or food and every move I made to create awareness about my books, speaking, or any of my entrepreneurial endeavors never seemed to succeed.

On this particular occasion, the bitterness I felt towards the selfish actions of one of my family members refused to subside. The anger that I felt burned me to the core so in an effort to release all those feelings without gossiping and causing discord, I released almost every emotion by way of this poem and incidentally upon completion I instantly felt better.

UNWORTHY

You say I am not good enough
That I'm barely deserving.
Therefore, should I let it matter
That you think so lowly of me?
You believe me to be nothing, barely worthy,
because you see no great measure of value in me,
So I must truly be undeserving.
Well, strangely enough,
I was inclined to agree.
Until I realized I was being indoctrinated
By a person who never themselves succeeded,
Go ahead, have your negative view,
But No longer will it control me.
For my dreams are like a lion
And they roar within me,
So today be put on notice
For I am not ashamed
Of the struggle that once controlled me
Because yesterday's sorrow has become my daily
testimony.

My life did not stop because I made the decision to pursue greater for my life. If anything, everything became more hectic. I once heard the saying "More money, more problems." Well, I was inclined to disagree as I seemed to experience the opposite effect, which went something like "no money, nothing but problems." Have you ever been in a relationship with a person whose family had what seemed to be an instant dislike towards you? Well, I certainly did!

For whatever reason, which was never shared with me directly, I was thought to be a hindrance to this guy that I loved and wanted to spend the rest of my life with just because some of his siblings felt I was not good enough.

To be fair, I was struggling due to the decision I made to pursue the dream to a reality full-time. However, that should never be a justification to despise anyone. So out of hurt, a little dejection, and eventual empowerment I released the pain I felt concerning that situation by way of the above poem.

DREAM KILLER

Have you ever been told you're not good enough?
That the path you're on is too ambiguous?
Constantly, they tell you what you should pursue
Is the path that's already paved for you.
Redundantly, they remind you of all your inadequacies,
Ever surmising your lack of successes
Perpetually squashing every dream you cling to.
Don't be swayed by their negative yet logical views;
Just girt yourself and get on your q's.
No matter how difficult it might be for you,
Let their words roll completely off of you.
For what they see is a result of no vision,
Blinded by the restrictions of their own inhibitions

Don't be bothered by what others may think of you for God has the last say!

Here is one of the things I have learned on this journey, people will, for no reason other than I assume bitterness due to their inability to achieve their own dreams, impose their negative views onto you. However, refuse to allow those logical dream killing words to sway you.

YOU HAVE NO IDEA

When you look at me
What do you perceive?
A girl?
A lady?
Maybe someone in need?
Yet I can't help but wonder,
Why you are unable to see
The strength that is undoubtedly me.
Thick lips, brown skin, and some hooped earrings,
But that should never be the factor
That determines the character
Of the inner me.

There are those who will never see you for the person you currently are for they are too focused on the person you used to be. I have been deemed worthy or unworthy based upon my financial straits, my choices, my appearance, even my age, however, none of the above should ever determine one's worth.

Life circumstances have the ability to either welcome you or chew you up and spit you out. It is for that reason you must be confident in who you are as an individual for it is virtually impossible to be everything to everyone.

This poem was written at a point in time of my life when I felt I was being subjected to undue and unfair scrutiny because of my lack of wealth, notoriety, and the color of my skin not from any outside races but my own.

I am most thankful to the Lord for teaching me that I am so much more than the struggle that was before me, and I am more than the image that precedes me

STRENGTH IN THE MIDST

No, I can't encourage you
When I need to be uplifted.
My life is in shambles and upside down,
Totally falling to pieces.
Daily you call me to suck me dry,
So that you can leave refreshed
While I'm left high and dry.
No, I can't! Not today,
Make you feel good in any way.
But in my head those thoughts remain,
For when the phone rings, I pick it up anyway.

Though this journey has at times been tumultuous and difficult to bear, in that moment, I was filled with uncertainty and much doubt. Everything around me seemed to be rapidly falling to pieces. I needed reassurance and encouragement that everything would be okay; however, one does not always get what they ask for in the way they hope to receive it.

Although on several occasions I have been encouraged by loved ones and strangers alike, it just so happened that the encouragement I desired did not come when and how I expected it.

AHLUMBA HARRIS

HOW MUCH LONGER

There is purpose to your pain, struggle, or loss so don't stop believing. To endure and sacrifice for so long just to give up right before you achieve victory should never be an option.
~Ahlumba

AHLUMBA HARRIS

REMAIN THE COURSE

In a split of a second, I became nervous.
Is what I have to offer really worth it?
Out of all my hard work
And all my personal loss,
Am I not also as deserving?
So, why do I occasionally feel that I am unworthy
Of the favor He behooved himself to show me?
Favor is kind. Favor is unmoving.
Yet I willingly allow these jitters to control me.
How much longer will I let anxiety rule me?
For in doing so, I put myself in jeopardy
Of blocking or losing
The gift God saw fit to bestow upon me.

I felt as if I was constantly at war with myself. Nothing I did seemed to be good enough. The endless adversity that I faced was wearing me down. The life that was evident before me was bleak with every shred of hope squashed. It was as if struggle with no lasting reprieve was assigned to my life.

Because I lacked so much and needed even more, I began to equate my lack of financial success with failure in life. Every lost opportunity, closed door, unanswered call, and false lead encountered weakened my resolve and belief that I would one day succeed. In my sorrow, I lost focus and forgot where the Lord had brought me from. I lost sight of the fact that he saw fit to not only gift me with purpose but to allow me the knowledge of what that purpose was.

Although I constantly begrudge the struggle and hardship I previously encountered, I can't help but realize that without those experiences, I would not be the person I am nor granted the opportunities I now walk in today.

I WONDERED WHY?

Why do you hold on?
I asked myself.
Why do you continue to reach for
The unseen this dream
Puzzled, I stared,
Unable to flow
Could it be that I did not know?
Everything was different,
Hard was an understatement.
Support? what a joke!
Starving artist was the only life
That I seemed to know.
Then I shifted my head,
Saw the work of my hands,
And thought, could it be
That all three came from me?
This gift that He bestowed upon me
Could not possibly be in vain
Yet it has become increasingly difficult
To hold through the dawn
When my life shows the fruit of eternal rain.
Every ending does not end with a smile.

But today, I do it by faith
Because that is the only way I know how.

Overcome with the evidence of no success or positive increase in my life, I began to doubt my abilities. I could no longer pinpoint why I was doing what I was doing, for it seemed no one was receptive to my efforts. The sales of my books were very inconsistent; I needed money and was at the beginning stages of losing what little I had left.

On this particular day, I was sitting at my desk crying due to all the stress when I happened to turn my head to the left and saw not one, not two, but three books written by my hand and I thought, "This has to be for some purpose."

The Lord would not have allowed me to write these books only to allow nothing to come of it. I was in way too deep, and had put too much of myself into this journey to give up now. So I let the tears continue to flow, smiled weakly, and continued to allow the words that bubbled up to flow out.

PRESS ON

It took fight for me to keep going,
To push through all the fears that tried to control me.
Lack and struggle, yeah, all the norms,
Played upon me like I was an accordion.
From day to day, yes, even nights,
I could never seem to burst through my plight.
So on and on and on I went,
Hoping for some betterment.
Only to be daily met
With the same old constant impediment.

My life sucked. I was lonely and did not understand why me achieving any financial goals was taking so long. Everything was so hard, and I could not figure out what I was doing wrong. I had a body of work, a website, social media pages, and was constantly reaching out to individuals, I even had my book in a brick and mortar building… yet, I still had nothing.

YOU NEED ME...NOT I YOU

Sit tight little Girl, keep your mouth shut,
You're the one that needs help not any of us.
Do what you are told. Jump when I say
Or be in jeopardy of me taking all my help away.
Sit tight little girl, yes, now you see,
I hold the key to what you currently need.
So all that I say is right and what you feel is wrong
because when you are the one in need
You are expected to have no spleen.

Kindness, generosity, and help should be given with no strings attached, but that is not always the case. There has been many a day that I have been on the receiving end of someone else's charity due to having a need that I was unable to fulfill for myself.

Though I was always happy and relieved to receive the help, my heart would be heavy for I felt that I had to jump through constant hoops just to make the person who was helping me feel good.

TRUST & BELIEVE

I have lived through each struggle,
Felt every pain,
Cried many tears due to the constant rain.
Why was this happening?
Where was my gain?
Left with no answers I turned to my faith,
For it was all that remained.
Why Lord? I asked.
I needed to know.
Yet, unfortunately, He seemed
To ignore my request.
Why? I asked again,
For surely He would see
That I could not have possibly deserved
All this that was happening to me.
So I shouted angrily again with my request,
But still He refused to answer me.
Nonetheless, my cry went unanswered.
Left wondering, with no rest,
I felt there was nothing left.

Sometimes you don't hear what you want. You don't see

what you need and don't get what you ask for. Does that mean that the Lord loves you any less or that He does not hear your plea? No, it just means that sometimes you have to believe by faith that there is a purpose and reason for it all. Sometimes the struggle that you experience is only to strengthen you in areas where you are weak.

Every end to a day will not always be a happy or easy one. Yet, despite the adversity you may face, it is imperative that you continue to believe, trust, and have faith not only in God's ability but also in your own.

This poem depicts my uncertainty in not only myself but also God. I was consumed with worry, fear, hurt, doubt, anger, and disbelief. There were many occasions I wanted to give up on persevering to be a successful author, a successful entrepreneur, and financially independent. Nevertheless, I made the choice to believe in God and the possibilities of my "one day."

SHAMED BY NEED

The day I had to accept government assistance
Was the day that I greatly resisted.
But the pain of our hunger would not go away,
So I made the choice to use it anyway.
Yes, I was embarrassed.
How could I not be?
But the Lord helped me to see
That it would bring my family
Some much needed relief.
So yes, I know what it is to be
Down, without, and yet fighting to be.
At times, the going would get so tough,
It became hard for me to believe in the dream
That burned so inside of me.

For years, I have felt as if I was in a constant financial drought. Surrounded by bills that I was unable to pay, on the verge of mental collapse, and barely able to eat I came to the realization that my pride was not helping me. I needed help, so I made the decision to apply for food stamps. It was one of the hardest decisions I had ever made in my adult life.

Determined to overcome my financial straits I refused to

allow those food stamps to be a crutch. Once the six month period ended, I was given the opportunity to have my case reviewed, which would enable the assistance to continue for an additional six months. Needless to relay, I happily canceled.

When you choose to pursue a more prosperous victorious life there will be things set before you that give evidence of defeat and habitual struggle; however, you must not allow any of that to deter you. Keep your course, keep your dream alive, and keep your vision before you by never losing track of what was placed in your heart.

Below I share one of my favorite scriptures:

Jeremiah 29:11 NIV *states: "For I know the plans I have for you," declares the Lord, "plans to prosper you and not to harm you, plans to give you hope and a future.*

For I know the thoughts that I think toward you, saith the Lord, thoughts of peace, and not of evil, to give you an expected end." ***Jeremiah 29:11 KJV***

WILL IT EVER BE

I dreamed a dream.
And occasionally that dream
Seemed far from me.
My head is just above the water.
My eyes barely able to see.
My breath, I continue to hold
Because I never know what's happening to me.
In one instant, I'm alive.
In another all there seems to be
Is an habitual dead end
That won't stop following me.
Dare to dream, I have said.
But what happens when that dream you dreamed
Continues to ever be
A floating aberration that will never be?

All I ever seemed to do was hope with no consistent results. False start after false start would consistently wear my spirit down. I awakened to the daily promise of potential possibilities only to end the night with my dreams even further out of reach than they were the night before.

I began to doubt if possible would ever be possible. With a heavy but hopeful heart, I once again chose to believe.

COULD NOT

My need was so great
I could barely celebrate
The victories the Lord saw fit
For me to effectuate.
All I could wonder
Was how would I acquire
What seemed to ever yet never be
Readily available to me.
That green, that cream,
That ever elusive means
That seemed to determine
If you really did succeed.
I breathe, I see, I perceive
With every bit of my being,
Every wandering dream,
that's inside of me.
Yet it doesn't see, hear or know of me.
It is for that reason, my constant need
For that monetary green, I fear my dreams
Will forever be out of my league.

Something good happened to me, but could I really

celebrate when I still needed so much more? Would this be an ongoing victory or one that ended where it began?

Therein lay the problem, I didn't know I wanted to believe that it would just be uphill from here but my heart had already taken so many hits that I couldn't truly release the joy because I was afraid. I was afraid of never having the opportunity to habitually achieve.

AHLUMBA HARRIS

KEEP THE FAITH

Though I am tired, I will continue to push myself, for my dream will only be seen if I have the continued discipline to achieve.
~Ahlumba

AHLUMBA HARRIS

FRESH START

Broken was the word that came to me,
Tired were the feet that could find no relief,
Hopeful was the heart that continued to believe,
Empty were the eyes that shed their last tears of defeat.
For the day that I decided to begin anew
Was the day that my life began to renew.
Nothing changed, not immediately,
Just the words from my mouth
And the perspective of my heart.
Before, I was filled with negativity,
Now all I can see are possibilities.
Survive, make it, or barely exist
Were the words that I refused to persist.
Life is a gift and I am determined to live it.
For we all have a journey,
And I implore you to embrace it.
Or will you decide to continue to just make it?

I could not help but believe that the winds of success, achievement, and victory were blowing in my direction. As I relayed in the poem above, nothing major changed; however something had changed. As always continued to believe.

COLLEAGUES WE WILL BE

I saw you for whom you would one day be,
But all you could see was the wrong
That apparently was me.
You said within the years
I have drained you dry,
Made constant bad decisions;
Basically, done nothing with my life.
It amazes me that I could
Apparently be in such desperate need
that I would receive
All the mess you dealt towards me.
Well, today I stand absolute,
Determined to be resolute.
Yes, you were a great support,
For I thought you gave from the heart.
Never did I imagine
that every dollar you handed
Was causing us to be disbanded.
With nothing else for me to do,
I have decided to release myself
From the shackle that is you.
No more will I be the hindering factor

That you obviously believe to be the one
Who single-handily caused you to be a nonfactor.

What greater gift can one receive than the correction of their erroneous beliefs? On my birthday (of all days), it was brought to my attention that the person that I believed to have supported me freely and with good will thought I was nothing but a hindrance to his growth and success as a person.

Disenchanted, hurt, and somewhat angry I released the pain that I felt in that moment by way of the above poem.

THINK NO LESS OF ME

I remember being in the midst of my sorrow,
Unable to realize the greatness
Jesus bestowed upon me
Constantly I wondered, "How would I make it?"
When All I could see
Was the destruction that was me.
How would I maintain
When I could barely sustain?
Work, I guess, is what I will do.
I will get me a job.
Yes, do what I have to do.
Does that mean I'm any less of a writer?
No, it's testament that when the going got tough
I was willing to keep fighting.

I was about to lose everything. I could not stay afloat because I was underwater. I was working hard yet I received no return. To find some relief, I continually repeated the proverb, "in all labor there is profit" because I believed the Lord's word to be true. But my life was not showing any profit.

I left my job. I had no money. And no matter what I did,

no doors would open. Things came to an ugly head when the water in my home was disconnected. For an entire day, we were without water and I was determined never to allow that to happen again. For that reason I became even more determined to rectify my financial straits.

I had to do something! I applied to several jobs (Macy's being my top choice). After a lot of follow through and persistence, I was finally hired part-time. Once I began working a traditional job, I began to think of myself as a farce; however, writing this freed me of those thoughts by helping me to realize that instead of giving up on my dream I simply found a way to continue to pursue them.

NEVER AGAIN!

> I tell you it has not been easy
> To stand tall when I have felt so uneasy.
> But fight I must to keep going
> Because I can't ever again let my circumstances
> Be allowed to control me.

Fight is what I have learned to do. No, I did not literally ball up a fist and go to blows with someone; I fought by way of sacrifice, endurance, faith, patience, and a refusal to give up. The mental weight of "will I ever" constantly weighed on me.

Physical, mental, and spiritual faith strength and wellness is needed when one makes the decision to pursue anything greater and outside the normal for their life. Doubt is a monster that is a spreadable contagion and if not checked has the ability to kill faith, dreams, hope, and ability.

IT'S TURNING AROUND

When once all I could do was believe unseen, He made it a reality so that I could not only hope but also could receive and achieve.
~Ahlumba

AHLUMBA HARRIS

UNABLE

I found myself lost without a cause,
On the brink, but unable to fall.
Do I keep going or will I let go
of all the hopes and dreams that kept me afloat?
On the verge of giving up,
I lifted my voice and gave it all up.
All the worry, all the fear,
and all the doubts of my yesteryear.
Now I sit contemplating
on how the Lord allowed me to make it.
Though struggles still rise to trouble me,
it is due to the strength
That He has given me
that the struggle no longer has the power
To trouble me.

Everything I believed to be true seemed to be false. Every move I made was returned with greater financial loss. I did not know what to believe anymore. It was not until later that I realized one must bear their own cross. Nothing worth its weight was going to be attained easily.

While experiencing the sting of lack, I could not appreciate the value of it. However, it is because of my willingness to go on a journey that I now have a story to tell.

I LOOKED AND SAW ME

I looked in the mirror
And I saw me.
I was no longer the fat me,
But the pretty me.
Now I would be happy.
Now I would be free.
But boy was I surprised
When that did not happen initially.
See, I thought that having a better outer
Would change my inner
When it was the transformation of my inner
That allowed me to see
That the beauty I constantly failed to see
Was already in me.

Sometimes we judge our worth by what appears on the outside without realizing that success, beauty, wealth, happiness, and life are inside of you. Don't wait until everything is dressed up all pretty with a bow before you realize your ability to win.

We all need to have the boldness and willingness to look beyond what is perceived as ugly, useless, insufficient, and inadequate to realize that it was not our stumbling block but our actual stepping stone to success.

What another believes does not have to be. So whether you believe or not, it is happening... Whether you agree or disagree, it is already being done.

ONCE THERE WAS NONE

I am filled with joy
When once there was only pain.
I believe things are looking up
Though it seems to be the same.
Something is different.
There has truly been a change,
For my heart has been uplifted,
And my old perspective no longer remains.
Thank you, Lord, for providing for me.
Thank you for another chance.
Though I have no clue what you have in store for me,
I can't help but impart this praise that's within
my heart.

After experiencing so much sorrow, it was imperative that I offer praise and thanks to the Lord for the joy that he placed in my heart and the peace of understanding that only He could give.

THE DAWN IS WHAT I SEE

The Lord just allowed me to see
So many possibilities.
This light that is my life
Has brightened significantly.
Has anything changed?
No, not much.
Just the constant negative focus
Of my wayward thoughts.
How good it feels to believe
When all I once did was cleave
To the doubt, fear, and disbelief
That for so long tormented me.

Everything was getting better. The pursuit of my entrepreneur endeavors was bringing forth more financial substance than it ever had. Doors were slowly creaking open, seeds that I had previously planted and forgotten had obviously taken root for I was beginning to receive. I was not where I envisioned, but things most certainly were turning around.

NO ONE BUT ME

God had a plan for me,
And I didn't know it.
Constantly, I complained.
So how could He show it?
My words were a cesspool of negativity.
Yet I had the nerve to doubt His ability.
I was the blame for my failures
Because I wanted a quick fix
When the Lord was trying to gift me with forever.
Convicted, I was to change my perspective,
And in doing so I received life anew
and joy everlasting.

I found fault in a little bit of everything because I was always focusing on others, who seemed to be achieving their dreams and goals at a much greater rate of speed than I was. Due to my refusal to remain focused and in my lane, I began to blame God.

THANKSGIVING

On this day of thanks be filled with joy.
Embrace your family and the love they share,
For there are those that are less fortunate,
Who are out there sad with no one to care.
It's not about shopping
Or the plentiful food at hand,
It is the agape love of thankfulness
that we are blessed to share.
So find someone that you know is feeling alone
due to their family being long gone,
and offer up what was thought to be lost;
A dwelling bursting with love, joy,
and yes, good food would be a plus.

Overwhelmed with the blessing that is family, I realized how blessed I was to not only be alive and healthy but to be surrounded by a wonderful daughter, spectacular siblings, and both my parents.

This helped me to better understand why my eldest sister always opened her home to strangers. It was so that they could have a taste of what we were blessed to have on a regular basis… a daily thanksgiving of togetherness.

IDLE HEART

I have been moved to take a stand
Against every sleeping woman or man.
Open your eyes, so you will see
The sleeping giant lying dormant in you.
A teacher, singer or a writer like me
Are just a few things that you could be.
But instead, you choose to live out your days
Working for another man while he gets paid.
Stop hiding your gifts, talents, and hopes
Behind the pretenses of a few jokes.
Get up, I say!
You sleeping woman or man,
Or forever lie dormant
Meaning you lie forever Broke.

In my everyday life, I have encountered some pretty extraordinary people doing some bare minimum ordinary things, which never fail to blow my mind with righteous indignation. All I see is wasted talent on an individual that refuses to step out on faith because they are too afraid to lose without realizing they have already lost.

SLEEPING GIANT

Did you not know
There is a gift lying dormant in you?
What is possible for one,
Is surely possible for you.
Don't give up because you cannot see it,
For the things worth having are hidden deeply
Kept under great safe-keeping.
So take the time to seek out your treasure,
For what God has given to you
Is certainly beyond measure.

It became evident to me many years ago when I was yet homeless, jobless, and feeling hopeless that there was something more to me than the habitual struggle I lived. For at that time all I excelled at was failing but I was determined to have more, to be more, and to do more.

I longed for a greater future. However a better life was not going to happen just because I hoped for it. I had to be willing to put in the work, push through the difficulties, and maintain during the sorrow while yet in the pursuit of the greatness that I envisioned for my life. The ongoing pain I felt, and the unshakable longing for more was part of the process. The pain was worth the gain.

Change What You See

When you Look in the mirror
What is it you see?
Could it be forgotten hopes, broken dreams
maybe some instability?
Girt yourself, hold your head high
For whatever you see has yet to be seen.
So turn the tide, begin anew,
And soon that mirror will be smiling at you

What we see does not have to actually be. You don't have to remain unhappy. You don't have to remain broke. You don't have to remain fat. You don't have to be lonely. You don't have to be abused.

Every day is a new opportunity to change your point of view therefore creating the catalyst to change the current destruction you live to a life for the better.

NEVER GIVE UP

Though I am tired I will continue to push myself, for my dream will only be seen if I have the continued discipline to achieve.
~Ahlumba

EVERYTHING HAS A BEGINNING

There is no greater struggle than being faced with what could have been. July 2013, I made the major decision to step out in faith and pursue what I believed to be my purpose.

Leading up to that decision I took my past and present circumstances into consideration and did not like what I saw. My life was going nowhere; I was unhappy, worked at a dead end job, and all I ever seemed to do was struggle. I had become the status quo; I hated my job, lived a mediocre life, and could not seem to get it together. I was the working poor.

Daily things seemed to get worse for me. I had trouble in my personal life, disappointments in my lack of career achievements, and I constantly yo-yoed in my spiritual life. My home life was an ongoing battle of never enough. I was tired with only one thing left to keep me going. Hidden deep in the recesses of my heart was the hope that maybe if I had faith and was bold enough to pursue my dream then maybe my dream would become more than a figment of my thoughts.

With the words of "It is possible" from individuals such as Joyce Meyer, Joel Osteen, T D Jakes, Les Brown, Eric Thomas, and Jamal Bryant ringing in my ear, and the plethora of books on faith I read (too many to recount) dancing through my head, I could not help but have the field of dreams mentality. While at work, church, home or anywhere, I stayed immersed in stories of triumph for I believed if the Lord did it for one would He not do much more for me.

When the time came for me to do or die, I was beyond ready to fly. The choice I made to leave my job was a very empowering one, and if it were not for the need for money, I would say it was the right one. With all my zest, eagerness, and desire to achieve success, I was in no way prepared for the difficulty I would encounter while working towards achieving my dream. For I was under the impression that despite how difficult or impossible it seemed; surely, I would eventually succeed.

When I read an inspirational book, heard a speech, or watched a video, the success was always spoken of in great detail however the struggle not as much. Words such as hard, difficult, not easy, tough were always used. However, in no way do those words (or any words for that matter) accurately describe the difficulty that is the pursuit of greatness.

You will be told to stay positive, don't give up, God won't leave you, you can do it, it's darkest before the dawn, and trouble won't last forever when you are faced with eviction, foreclosure, an inability to pay bills, no insurance, no water, no electricity, no food, and no money until eventually you are left with no hope.

I thought the hardest part of my journey was over two books ago but boy was I wrong. Never did I imagine an even greater struggle would be before me. When I left my job, things were better yet worse. I was empowered, I was happy, I had a plan, and I was going to live my dream but more doors remained closed than the ones that opened.

Diligently, I planted seeds with the hope that one day I would receive. Instead, I encountered numerous closed doors, hundreds of unanswered emails, many unreturned phone calls, several dead ends gone down, and tons of material given with nothing to show for it but a whole lot of "yes, I will support you!" with no follow through.

It was during the times of difficulty that I had to fight to remain the course. I fought through the gift of writing that the Lord gave me, my faith, and my continued perseverance. For the urgent desire to achieve and accomplish something greater refused to subside. As a result, I continued to work hard and write, for writing was how I let go. It helped me put into perspective that no matter what appeared to be my failures, I could not give up my passion.

As time passed and my struggle refused to cease, I once

again became angry. I questioned why I should continue on when I seemed to reap no reward. I did not want to write, I wanted to let go, but the words inside of me refused to be ignored. I was tired of all the false hope and continued let downs.

In forced obedience, I wrote daily, but I had very little hope. My days began to blend into one. I had nothing, I felt like nothing. Therefore, I thought I was nothing. I began to doubt the validity of my existence. That was a major sign that I needed to strengthen the relationship that I allowed to weaken with God, so I began to pray, fast, and read my bible. I also began to listen to some powerful praise and worship music that really breathed life not only to my dying spirit but also to the current situation of defeat that I was experiencing.

It was during my time of worship that some wonderful things began to happen. My spirit was reawakened, and I was reminded of who I was. Slowly my perspective began to change, and I began to believe that everything was going to turn around for the better. Never did I imagine that the words "now my journey begins" that I ended my very first book "Inspired2prosper" with would not only be prophetic but also would turn around and kick me in the butt several times.

Though it's never been claimed that anything worth having can be obtained easily, that does not mean I expected to travel down a road that had no direction. Many days I became discouraged with feelings of defeat that almost were successful in overtaking the desire I had to succeed. However the Lord always put someone or thing in my path to keep alive the seed that was planted in me years ago, even when I thought it to be dead.

I know what it is to have a strong inclination that there is more to you than what initially meets the eye of others, yet the life that you currently live fails to show it. I know what it is like to constantly give support and never seem to receive it. I know what it feels like to cry because the loneliness of your journey makes you feel like it is too much to bear.

I have experienced doubt and disbelief in my own capability, brought on by fear due to what I did not see. But in order for the negative to change, I had to alter the perspective of my view. As long as I had one bit of belief that I could succeed, it was imperative that I continued to do my part to achieve it. In challenging myself to be positive, I realized how negative I was. In choosing to speak life, I was faced with how speaking death gave life to negativity.

Faith is the substance of things hoped for, evidence unseen, so stop speaking continuous life to what is already evident yet unwanted. Faith requires that we have the Boldness and belief to speak life to a dying situation, when what we see shows proof of defeat, lack, sickness, loss, loneliness, even heartache. Stop perpetuating what already is and begin speaking fearlessly what you would like it to be.

I chose to take the road less traveled, I was willing to risk and lose it all to pursue and invest into one of the greatest things that I could have ever been given: my life. How I chose to go about making my dream a reality will not likely be the way you choose to pursue your own; however, if you have not already done so, I encourage you to set that captive dream, desire, goal or vision for your life free.

Trouble will come. However, no matter how that trouble causes you to feel, you must continue to believe that you can achieve the dream or vision God instilled in you. Anything worth achieving takes time, strength, and a whole lot of patience

"Life does not cease to exist because one made the decision to give up."

You are probably thinking this has been a hellacious journey for her, why would I ever want to put myself through the same? If that is your thought then the only response I have is one who wants more does not have to be persuaded to obtain it.

I made the mistake of believing that just because I struggled that I had failed. In order to win one at some point must fail.

Don't allow your possible or impossible dreams be swayed by the failures of others for there are several stories out there of individuals who successfully achieved the impossible against insurmountable odds. Never make a decision solely on what another claims to be possible, for the word impossible is the state of another's mind of thought.

If you believe in a thing it becomes your responsibility to strive towards achieving it. No matter the resistance I encountered I continued to move forward. When I began to work at Macy's part time I still continued to fight for my success, when I was on food stamps I fought for my dream. When I almost lost my home the Lord refused to allow me to be defeated.

I never gave up even when the circumstances that surrounded me showed only lack and defeat. I continued to soldier forward until one by one the shackles of lack, and the bonds of struggle slowly began to release.

Everything has a beginning...Only you determine the ending.

CAN'T GET ENOUGH?

Visit:
www.ahlumba.com

www.facebook.com/ahlumbah

SHARE YOUR STORY WITH US

Have you obtained some personal success? Why not share it with us?
Don't worry know success is ever to small to share, we want to celebrate with you…

www.inspired2prosper.com

If you have any questions, concerns, or inspiring words, please feel free to contact us at:

CONTACTUS@INSPIRED2PROSPER.COM

FEEL FREE TO CHECK OUT AHLUMBA'S NATURAL PRODUCT LINE:

WWW.OMYPRODUCTS.COM

AHLUMBA HARRIS

AHLUMBA

Ahlumba Harris; a high school dropout, a college dropout, and a single mother of one who had the fortitude to search for and obtain more despite the mediocrity that tried to contain her. Just like you she constantly seeks to improve her physical, spiritual, and financial wellbeing for she is in a journey to reach her destiny…

www.ingramcontent.com/pod-product-compliance
Lightning Source LLC
Chambersburg PA
CBHW032206040426
42449CB00005B/468